Having an Iron Will

David M. Blunt

© 2001 by David M. Blunt

Having an Iron Will
by David M. Blunt

Printed in the United States of America
ISBN 1-931232-16-4

All rights reserved. No part of this publication may be reproduced or transmitted in any form or by any means without written permission of the publisher.

Xulon Press
344 Maple Ave. West, #302
Vienna, VA 22180
703-691-7595
XulonPress.com

Table of Contents

Introduction... 1

Chapter 1—Strength of Will Determines Scope of
     Possibilities.............................. 3

Chapter 2—You Must Be Stronger Than Your
     Obstacles................................ 31

Chapter 3—Problems Are the Seeds of Promotion...... 55

Introduction

Having an **Iron Will** is not an option if you are serious about being a Christian. Walking in the power of the Spirit requires it, as does being in the forefront of today's issues.

Confronting the believer are multitudes of choices – some good and some bad. These choices bring every Christian to the brink of their Christianity at some point or another, and their strength of character or **Iron Will** is what brings them through.

Success in life is not measured by the absence of difficulty. Success in life is overcoming the difficulties you face with dignity and emerging with your integrity intact. The development of an **Iron Will** is the primary weapon for you to use against the power of the enemy, and this book will help you develop it.

Read on if you desire to move to the next level of your Christian walk. I assure you, you will not regret it.

He that overcometh shall inherit all things; and I will be his God, and he shall be my son.

(Revelation 21:7 KJV)

Chapter 1

Strength of Will Determines Scope of Possibilities

Ram and Kong were pushed toward the crowd awaiting them. They had just been "arrested" for trying to convert people to Christianity, and now the mob wanted them. What their fate would be was in the hands of God; they had no control.

Suddenly, a rock shot out of the middle of the throng and hit Ram in the chest. "Would this be how it ends?" he wondered.

"Stand tall, Ram!" Kong shouted. "You can do anything in Christ!"

The leader of the mob shouted at Ram and Kong to renounce their faith and deny Jesus. With one voice, both men proclaimed that Jesus is Lord and they would never betray Him.

The beating continued and both Ram and Kong floated in and out of consciousness. Then

Kong began to speak: "Men and brothers! What are you doing? Don't you see that this hatred and murder is wrong and does nothing but cause pain? We are your brothers, and we love you. Jesus sent us to tell you that He loves you too and gave up His life to save you. Jesus governs with love; peace is found at His feet. Hear Him today and turn from this violence!"

The mob fell silent. The only sound was the raspy breathing of two nearly dead men. As one, the crowd turned away and left the men there — their ordeal was over as quickly as it began.

Family by family, the entire village came to know Jesus. They had seen Him on the road the day that Ram and Kong were nearly killed. Never before had they seen such love expressed in *the midst of brutality.*

What does it mean to have an "Iron Will?"

And it came to pass, when the time was come that he should be received up, he steadfastly set his face to go to Jerusalem…

(Luke 9:51)

Jesus life was marked by this decision to go to Jerusalem. He knew that death awaited Him, yet He *"steadfastly set His face"* toward His destiny. Throughout the Bible, we see men and women who demonstrated what it meant to have an **Iron Will**. Their resolution and dedication to the cause or task at hand spoke volumes about their strength of character.

What is an **Iron Will**? Definitions include:

- Willpower

- Staying power

- Power to hold on

- Power to stand fast

- Determination

- Courage

- Persistence

A person with an **Iron Will** is unstoppable and unbreakable. To them, it's always too soon to quit because in the face of persistence, difficulties disappear and obstacles turn into opportunities.

Consider the three Hebrew children of Daniel chapter 3, Shadrach, Meshach, and Abednego. King Nebuchadnezzar had a statue built in his honor, and required all the people of Babylon to bow and worship it. Shadrach, Meshach, and Abednego refused saying it violated their allegiance to Jehovah.

The king was furious and demanded they worship or be thrown into a blazing furnace and be killed. Again, the three Hebrew boys stood firm and refused to bow down:

Shadrach, Meshach, and Abednego, answered and said to the king, O Nebuchadnezzar, we are not careful to answer thee in this matter. If it be so, our God whom we serve is able to deliver us from the burning fiery furnace, and he will deliver us out of thine hand, O king. But if not, be it known unto thee, O king, that we will not serve thy gods, nor worship the golden image which thou hast set up.

(Daniel 3:16-18)

Their resolve and persistence to do what was right in the sight of God forced the king's hand. Nebuchadnezzar had them thrown into the furnace intending to see them destroyed. However, the flames did them no harm and they emerged with not even the smell of smoke on their garments. This display of **Iron Will** was sufficient for the king to listen to the boys and worship God as well.

Persistence Makes The Impossible Possible

Charles Spurgeon said it was by perseverance that the snail reached Noah's Ark. Nothing takes the place of perseverance, and with it, nothing can stop you from crossing the finishing line – not pain, or circumstances, or criticisms.

The strength of your will determines the scope of your possibilities. If your will is weak, then fulfillment of the possibilities before you is limited. The Bible says that Jesus, *"for the joy that was set before him endured the cross"* (Hebrews 12:2). Because of His determination and resolve, salvation is available to all who desire it. That includes you! Jesus' joy is seeing you saved and living with Him for eternity.

You may be tempted to give up because the price of your dream may seem too great. However, the cost to stay where you are is far greater than moving toward fulfilling your dream. Staying the same without the willingness to make changes and move forward will bankrupt your soul.

Standing water is prone to stagnation. Left long enough, the water becomes putrid and unfit for consumption. People are the same way. Being stagnant in your life is a dreadful and dangerous way to be. If changes don't occur that allow fresh water to flow in, you will become putrid and unfit for anything. Your possibilities disappear and failure becomes your companion.

Stagnation is not God's will for you! God has deposited in you the perseverance of Jesus. Every born again believer has the Spirit of God living in them. This is the same Spirit that raised Jesus from the dead according to Romans 8:11, and the same Spirit that enabled Him to go through the cross.

And the very God of peace sanctify you wholly; and I pray God your whole spirit and soul and body be preserved blameless unto the coming of our Lord Jesus Christ.

(1 Thessalonians 5:23)

Belief Is an Act of the Will

Every believer is made up of 3 parts, spirit, soul and body; you are a spirit, you have a soul, and you live in a body. The realm of your soul is made up of the will, emotions, and intellect. Your soul is at the center of your being and your will is at the center of your soul. It is through your will that you interact with your environment. Yes, your senses contribute, but how you relate to what is around you is the result of your will – how you have decided to be.

Throughout Scripture, believers are encouraged to hold fast or hold on, and are repeatedly told not to be afraid. The act of holding fast and of not being afraid is determined by a decision that is a manifestation of **Iron Will**.

It's with your will that you believe and out of your will you make choices. That's what is meant by the phrase, "free will." Thomas had a choice to make regarding the resurrection of Jesus; would he believe or disbelieve what the others said. He is called "Doubting Thomas" because he chose to see for himself and not believe what the other disciples witnessed.

> *The other disciples therefore said unto him (Thomas), We have seen the Lord. But he said unto them,*
>
> *Except I shall see in his hands the print of the nails, and put my finger into the print of the nails, and thrust my hand into his side, I will not believe.*
>
> (John 20:25)

God gives you many choices in life to make, one of which is whether to serve Him or the devil. How you handle the choices God gives you determines the scope of your possibilities. If you choose not to follow Jesus, then how can you fulfill the possibilities that God has set before you? Your life is the sum total of all your choices, so it's out of your will that you choose to either stop or keep going. What is the joy set before you that will enable you to endure?

An Iron Will Has An Iron Grasp

It is vital for every believer to have a solid, strong, iron-like will. A person with **Iron Will** has an iron-like grasp and will not let go. They will not release their grip, but will cross the finish line to win the prize.

Elisha followed Elijah the prophet for years as a faithful and devoted disciple. Elisha knew that the mantle of Elijah's ministry would come to him so long as he persevered and stayed close. At one point, Elijah demanded that Elisha leave but Elisha refused: *"And Elijah said unto him, Tarry, I pray thee, here; for the LORD hath sent me to Jordan. And he (Elisha) said, As the LORD liveth, and as thy soul liveth, I will not leave thee. And they two went on"* (2 Kings 2:6).

A double portion of the ministry of Elijah was the reward of Elisha's determination. Elisha went on to become one of the most powerful prophets of God in the Bible. His exploits are legendary, and he had powerful impact on the people of his day. Elisha held on to Elijah with an iron grip, and wouldn't let the prophet go without a blessing (2 Kings 2:9)

A person with **Iron Will** has bulldog determination, persistence, and a fixed mindset. Their power to hold on is vital in overcoming…

- Calamity
- Criticism
- Opposition
- Defeat
- Discouragement

- Sadness
- Sickness
- Sorrow
- Strife
- Time
- Circles
- Obstacles

Nothing can stop a person with an **Iron Will**. They take misfortune and turn it into a fortune. They are unstoppable.

Eight Characteristics of Iron Will

*And beside this, giving all **diligence**, add to your faith **virtue**; and to virtue **knowledge**;*

*And to knowledge **temperance**; and to temperance **patience**; and to patience*

godliness;

And to godliness brotherly kindness; and to brotherly kindness **charity**.

For if these things be in you, and abound, they make you that ye shall neither be barren nor unfruitful in the knowledge of our Lord Jesus Christ.

But he that lacketh these things is blind, and cannot see afar off, and hath forgotten that he was purged from his old sins.

Wherefore the rather, brethren, give diligence to make your calling and election sure: for if ye do these things, ye shall never fall:

(2 Peter 1:5-10)

Characteristic #1: Diligence

You must work to succeed and not quit. Diligence means you are working when the others have gone home. It means that you go the extra mile to learn and become. It means that when everyone else has quit, you haven't. Diligence means you look after the details yet keep the big picture in mind. Diligence takes the extra step to ensure that something is done properly and completely – you never leave a job partially done. Add diligence to your faith and it will be fruitful; they are cooperating powers.

Characteristic #2: Virtue

Virtue is moral excellence in all things. Virtue is a characteristic of holiness and an attribute of God. To be virtuous is to be one of high integrity and honesty.

A woman was healed when she touched the hem of Jesus' garment (Luke 8:43-48). Jesus wanted to know who touched Him because He felt virtue flowing out of Him. This use of the word indicates there is power in virtue. The Greek word "dunamis" is translated "virtue" in the Scripture reference above, and can mean, "ability, able, meaning, might, mighty, miracle, power, strength, and strengthen." Therefore, to have virtue means you have strength, power, and ability, which are characteristics of **Iron Will**.

Iron Will is necessary at times to avoid the pitfalls of temptation placed before you. It enables you to be honest and of high integrity at all times whether alone or in the company of others.

Characteristic #3: Knowledge

Knowledge of who you are and whose you are is vital in the development of godly character. Believers must be immersed in the Word of God in order to fully understand His character. Out of that understanding comes the knowledge necessary to become what God intends you to become.

Characteristic #4: Temperance

Being balanced and self-controlled is paramount in cultivating an **Iron Will**. However, **Iron Will** can just as easily work against you, if it's out of balance you're either stubborn or you're obstinate. It's vital to be tempered by the Holy Spirit to avoid sin.

Characteristic #5: Patience

Iron Will brings with it perseverance to persist despite the obstacles.

> *My brethren, count it all joy when ye fall into divers temptations; Knowing this, that the trying of your faith worketh patience. But let patience have her perfect work, that ye may be perfect and entire, wanting nothing.*
>
> *(James 1:2-4)*

Patience will perfect you. It is a tool that believers must have at their disposal if they desire to overcome. **Iron Will** makes it possible to have patience.

Characteristic #6: Godliness

Godliness is the result of sanctification – living a life of faith and holiness. Being godly means that others can see the Father in you which draws them to Jesus. Another word for godly is righteous. Being righteous means being in right standing with God. Paul said this about righteousness, "*For he hath made him to be sin for us, who knew no sin; that we might be made the righteousness of God in him*" (2 Corinthians 5:21).

You are the righteousness of God in Christ! You are a godly one.

Iron Will is best expressed in godliness. There is no abuse of power or position when operating in subjection to the Holy Spirit through godliness.

Characteristic #7: Brotherly Kindness

Brotherly kindness relates to your relationship with other believers. How do you get along with others in the family of God?

We love him, because he first loved us. If a man say, I love God, and hateth his brother, he is a liar: for he that loveth not his brother whom he hath seen, how can he love God whom he hath not seen? And this commandment have we from him, That he who loveth God love his brother also.

(1 John 4:19-21)

Characteristic #8: Charity

Charity is an attitude of benevolence toward others that comes straight from the heart. Born out of the Father's love, charity looks out for the welfare of others. **Iron Will** must be filled with charity to guard against harshness or indifference.

Being aware of others was modeled perfectly by Jesus. Paul said, "*And now abideth faith, hope, charity, these three; but the greatest of these is charity"* (1 Corinthians 13:13).

Iron Will Causes Faith To Abound

Other words for "**Iron Will**" include: resolve, resolution, and determination. Add resolution—**Iron Will**—to your faith in order to finish and win the prize. Resolve to let nothing deter or defeat you. No matter what happens next week, hold on.

Now faith is the substance of things hoped for, the evidence of things not seen… But without faith it is impossible to please him: for he that cometh to God must believe that he is, and that he is a rewarder of them that diligently seek him… By faith Abraham, when he was called to go out into a place which he should after receive for an inheritance, obeyed; and he went out, not knowing whither he went. By faith he sojourned in the land of promise, as in a strange country, dwelling in tabernacles with Isaac and Jacob, the heirs with him of the same promise: For he looked for a city which hath foundations, whose builder and maker is God.

(Hebrews 11:1,6,8-10)

Your faith will be strengthened by your resolve to believe God. How else could you step out in faith if you had not resolved to believe what God said? When you are finally moved by faith that is supported by **Iron Will**, you will not stop nor will you quit. Difficulties will come but you resolve to be determined. **Iron Will** includes these components:

- Persistence
- Self-control

- Discipline

Fruit of The Spirit

> But *the fruit of the Spirit is love, joy, peace, long-suffering, gentleness, goodness, faithfulness, Meekness, temperance: against such there is no law.*
>
> (Galatians 5:22-23)

Self-control is recognized as a fruit of the Spirit. Because the Holy Spirit lives in you, self-control is automatically an attribute of your soul. You may need to develop it through exercise, but it is yours through the Spirit. Another fruit of the Spirit is long-suffering or patience. Both are required for you to have a will that won't quit.

Faith coupled with **Iron Will** is necessary for your

marriage to work, and to properly care for your children, especially teenagers. Because you have the fruit of the Spirit, you already have the components of an **Iron Will**.

The apostle Paul declared in 2 Timothy 1:7, *"For God hath not given us the spirit of fear; but of power, and of love, and of a sound mind."* The word "sound" in Greek means discipline. Your mind may not yet be fully renewed, but you do have the *spirit* of a disciplined mind; Jesus gave it to you.

Discipline enables you to be unbreakable, unstoppable, and unbeatable. It empowers you with the **Iron Will** necessary to get up in the midst of pain, lack of rest, and discomfort, and to cross the finish line to gain the prize.

Having an **Iron Will** means you are a person of discipline, self-control, and persistence. Pray this prayer out loud to ask God to develop an **Iron Will** more fully in you:

— David M. Blunt —

Heavenly Father, You are gracious and your mercy lasts forever. I ask you now to develop within me through your Holy Spirit an **Iron Will.** I want to be one You can depend on to do what You need done in my part of the world. Empower me, Lord, and strip away all that is not like You in my life. In Jesus' name. Amen.

Chapter 2

Your Want Must Be Stronger Than Your Obstacles

For twelve years, she had been confined to her home, only leaving the house when she went to see her physician. Living like a recluse, she had lost all contact with the community and had become an object of gossip and pity. Suffering from vaginal hemorrhaging, her resources were nearly as exhausted as her hope. Would this never end?

One day, she heard about a healer that was causing quite a stir among the people. "Could he help me?" she wondered. Weak and unable walk very far, she set out to see.

Suddenly a crowd of people was rushing toward her. Fearfully, she moved aside, unsure of what was happening. Then, she heard His name, "Jesus."

Something inside her began to stir. "I must touch Him!" she thought. "But how?" The crowd had become a throng with everyone pushing and shoving to get a better position.

Then, she saw Him. Jesus was moving through the crowd toward her! "Maybe," she thought, "I can get close enough to touch Him." With all her might, she pushed and struggled. The crowd pressed in even tighter as Jesus drew near, but she was determined not to let this opportunity pass.

Her strength was failing fast, and the heat of the crowd was making her dizzy. "Oh, Jesus!" she cried as she fell forward. Reaching as far as she could, she stretched her hand to touch the hem of His garment as He passed by; this was her only hope.

The moment the fabric touched her fingers, she felt power surge through her. She knew immediately that the flow of blood had stopped, and strength began to course through her body. Her heart was pounding and her mind was racing – she had been healed!

Then Jesus stopped, wanting to know who touched Him. As He scanned the crowd, His eyes locked on hers. The people backed away as Jesus lifted her to her feet. Looking into His eyes, the love and compassion she felt was beyond words. Mercy flooded over her and bathed her weary soul as she heard Jesus say: "Daughter. Your faith has made you whole"

(Luke 8: 49).

What Is The Story of Your Life?

Like the woman in the story above, your desire must be stronger than any obstacles, problems, or mountains. Desire is the seed bed of accomplishment, if it's strong enough, your…

- mountains become momentum makers
- problems become promotions
- weakness becomes strength

Desire takes you beyond your limitations and opens wide the doors of opportunity that lie before you. No longer are you held back by what you believed you could or could not do. Instead, new horizons and expanded vistas beckon, calling you to the future and destiny that is yours in Christ.

Desire makes it possible for you to stick to it until you arrive at your destination. You'll be like a biscuit that rises when it's exposed heat. You too, will rise to the occasion because you are a Holy Ghost, born again, Spirit-filled biscuit. You have an **Iron Will**.

You have the opportunity to create your own true-life story that will impact and encourage others. Now you can be the difference in someone else's life to help them be over comers. You have the power to make the story of your life one of motivation, inspiration, aspiration, and admiration.

Pressing on in the face of adversity develops character. Understanding your limitations is important, but knowing your destiny is of even greater importance. You may have weaknesses but Christ will fill in what you don't have. He is your all-sufficient source.

Everybody has been told at one time or another that what he or she was attempting would never happen and they would never be successful. However, those who persist in spite of the negative comments of others go on to success. Success doesn't just happen; it's the result of deliberate and persistent action.

Have you ever been told something would never happen but it did? Have you kept going in spite of the negativity and refused to give up, quit, or withdraw? If so, you showed your **Iron Will**.

God Changes The Value of Failure

There is no such thing as failure when you are in Christ. Yes, you will have setbacks and will face difficulty, but to fail is not possible. I'm sure you're wondering how I can say that in the face of your experience or that of others. It's very simple. To be in Christ is to be in the seat of authority over all things. This doesn't mean that you are running things because Jesus rules by His Word. However, you have been given dominion over the situations in your life (Genesis 1:26-27). To rule over them, you must be led by the Spirit of God (Romans 8:14).

To have an **Iron Will** is better than genius, talent, money, networking, or people skills. Take the attitude that you are always learning and can never loose at anything, then God can change your…

- pain to gain
- scars to stars
- mistakes to miracles
- wounds to wisdom
- loses into winnings

Are you growing in life, or does the least setback knock the wind out of you? You are either getting smaller or you are getting greater. John said, *"Ye are of God, little children, and have overcome them: because greater is he that is in you, than he that is in the world"* (1 John 4:4). Hold your course until it is done. Your life is a story being told and people are watching to see if you will finish.

"And let us not be weary in well doing: for in due season we shall reap, if we faint not" (Galatians 6:9). We discussed in the last chapter that the strength of your will determines the scope of your possibilities. Having a strong will doesn't mean that you are not teachable or won't learn from your mistakes. A strong will means that in the face of problems and adversity you, like Jesus, keep your face set in the direction God has called you to go.

Other people can confirm what God tells you, however, He sets the direction for your life, not them. Again, listen for confirmation but get your determination from God. Proverbs 16:9 declares, *"A man's heart deviseth his way: but the* LORD *directeth his steps."* It's OK to make a plan and it's OK to have direction, just let the Lord direct how the plan is implemented.

Invincible determination is the distinction between great men and little men. Calvin Coolidge said, *"Nothing can take the place of persistence."* This sentiment is echoed by Ross Perot, *"Most people give up when they are about to achieve success, one foot from the winning touch down."*

What about you? Are you willing to take another step to see the dream come true? Are you willing to tolerate the negativity of others to fulfill what God has set in your heart?

You Have What It Takes

The seed of greatness is planted inside of you. The Spirit of the living God dwells in you, which means that all the creativity of the universe is at your disposal. This is not to say that every believer will be great at everything. What I'm saying is that for whatever God has called you to do, you have the tools necessary to accomplish it.

You have what it takes on the inside no matter what's on the outside. It's an inside job requiring backbone and courage, not being a wimp with no purpose. Let courage be your coach. Scripture teaches you to be bold in what you do, so step out with confidence and see what God can do in and through you.

The Spirit of God inside you brings discipline and the fruit of self-control and persistence. Therefore, when the devil comes against you saying that against all the odds you can't make it, you know it is not the truth. You can do all things through Christ who strengthens you (Philippians 4:13). You can overcome all odds. You have what it takes on the inside; develop it.

The woman with the issue of blood in Luke 8 used what she had. Her determination and perseverance moved her to receive everything God had for her. It's interesting that because of her determination and perseverance she is immortalized in Scripture and used as an example to bring hope and strength to those who are weak. You never know when others will find strength and courage in seeing what you've overcome in your life. Don't be afraid of whether you'll succeed. Through Christ, you'll always make it through.

David was a young shepherd boy when he heard a loud, boisterous, giant of a man profane the name of God. His anger burned within him and he determined not to allow this heathen named Goliath to disparage God (1 Samuel 17). David had a heart after God. He worshiped God in all that he did, and was fearless in his service for the Lord.

When David went out to face the giant, he chose five smooth stones from a stream and loaded one into his sling. The giant was as blasphemous toward David as he was toward God, but David stood his ground. He told Goliath that God had delivered him into his hands that day, and that he would feed his carcass to the birds of the air.

Imagine for a moment the scene: David was a teenager, probably less than five feet in height while Goliath was over nine feet tall. Do you think the devil was trying to talk into David's ear about failure? Of course he was. Nevertheless, David had been given Goliath; all he had to do was collect him. The story goes on to relate how David killed the giant with only one stone and then cut off his head.

This is what it means to stay the course and keep focused on what God has called you to do. It's too easy to get sidetracked with all the commotion and things clamoring for your attention. Once you have the giant in your sight, take him out – that is the promise of God in your life. You've been given the five smooth stones, choose the one necessary to get the job done.

The Righteous Shall Hold His Way

You will never achieve your God given dream without an **Iron Will**. If what God has for you to do requires no effort, would it be worth your doing? Would you invest yourself in something that seemed shallow and of little consequence? When God gives you a dream, He gives you one that is worth reaching for.

Job 17:9 says, "*The righteous also shall hold on his way, and he that hath clean hands shall be stronger and stronger.*" This truth is awesome and very practical. Take this verse and mark it, circle it, claim it, name it, blab it, grab it, take it, make it, personalize it, and visualize it. See yourself as a person who does not give up.

You may have heard about the soldier that was the only one left alive in his unit. He was surrounded by hundreds of hostile forces and had no ammunition, only a bayonet. As the enemy moved in for the final battle, the soldier shouted at them that this was their last chance to surrender.

What kind of soldier are you? Are you one who gives up your weapon when the odds are stacked against you, or do you give the enemy one last chance to surrender?

The king of Aram was seeking to overthrow Israel, but

wanted to destroy Elisha first:

> And he said, Go and spy where he is, that I may send and fetch him. And it was told him, saying, Behold, he is in Dothan. Therefore sent he thither horses, and chariots, and a great host: and they came by night, and compassed the city about. And when the servant of the man of God was risen early, and gone forth, behold, an host compassed the city both with horses and chariots. And his servant said unto him, Alas, my master! how shall we do? And he answered, Fear not: for they that be with us are more than they that be with them. And Elisha prayed, and said, LORD, I pray thee, open his eyes, that he may see. And the LORD opened the eyes of the young man; and he saw: and, behold, the mountain

was full of horses and chariots of fire round about Elisha.

(2 Kings 6:13-17)

Often, Christians need to have their eyes opened to see who is on their side. The servant of Elisha was clueless until God showed him the forces of heaven arrayed against the enemy.

Where God Guides, God Provides

When God gives you a dream or sets you on a course, He ensures that all the resources of heaven necessary to bring it to pass are available to you. God will not leave you "high and dry." Moses was given a rod that could be used to turn water into blood, divide a sea, defeat the enemy, provide water, and more.

If God will do that with a rod in the hand of a faithful

servant, imagine what He will do with what He's given you!

You may think that whatever you have to use is inadequate for the task at hand. It's true. If it's only you and your tool, no matter what you do, it will probably not be enough. However, when God is put into the equation, conventional math goes out the window. God, plus whatever you have equals the power of the universe in your hand!

Knowing this, you will hold true to the course and will get continually stronger. You will live a life of integrity and character, and your cup will run over.

The apostle Paul went through trials the like of which most of us cannot relate at all:

> *Of the Jews five times received I forty stripes save one. Thrice was I beaten with rods, once was I*

stoned, thrice I suffered shipwreck, a night and a day I have been in the deep; In journeyings often, in perils of waters, in perils of robbers, in perils by mine own countrymen, in perils by the heathen, in perils in the city, in perils in the wilderness, in perils in the sea, in perils among false brethren; In weariness and painfulness, in watchings often, in hunger and thirst, in fastings often, in cold and nakedness.

(2 Corinthians 11:24-27)

Paul did not lose heart and give up because of all these trials. Instead, his faith became stronger and more vital. Paul discovered a profound principle of the gospel in the midst of these trials – the higher the heat, the closer you are to the flame. Just like the three Hebrew children, Shadrach, Meshach, and Abednego, Paul saw the power of God made manifest in his life.

You can do the same. Jesus said in Mark 9:49, *"For every one shall be salted with fire."* Are you willing to go through the fire to receive what God has for you? Are you willing to see the power of God made manifest in your life through difficulty, adversity, and trials? Do you want to experience firsthand the faithfulness of God?

Through righteousness, you can hold on if you keep your hands clean. You can overcome and achieve. You can rise above all odds and persist because you are the righteousness of God (2 Corinthians 5:21). You will see your…

- kids return from the enemies land
- marriage as it should be
- business started and successful
- ministry launched, living and enlarged

Don't give excuses, quit, or cash in. Hold on. Your 'Goliath' is a promotion in waiting. David would not have been known had it not been for one of his problems; Goliath was his promotion.

You reign in this life as the King's child. You will hold to your course because you have integrity and are becoming stronger and stronger. Discipline is a fruit of the Holy Spirit living inside of you, and being demonstrated on the outside.

You can be like the apostle Paul. After he told of all the trials and persecutions in 2 Corinthians 11, he penned this: *"Therefore I take pleasure in infirmities, in reproaches, in necessities, in persecutions, in distresses for Christ's sake: for when I am weak, then am I strong"* (2 Corinthians 12:10).

You get stronger because you recognize your weakness and where your strength comes from. Stand tall, because the God of the universe is your constant source of help in times of need.

Chapter 3

Problems Are the Seeds of Promotion

John ached for the chance to prove himself. He knew that he could do the job as well as anyone else in the company; all he needed was a chance.

Making parachutes for competitive skydivers was a very specialized job, one that John took very seriously. He had worked at ProChute for more than a decade, but felt frozen in place by the longevity of other, older employees. He had finally decided to give up on promotion because the only way it could happen was if his boss retired; and that was a long way off.

Still, John looked for ways to improve on the job. He also liked to experiment and find new, innovative ways to make the job easier or the product more durable.

One day, John was called into his supervisor's

office. A new, secret job was being awarded to the company. The person his boss had singled out to run the project was John. However, there was a problem. Six hundred specialized chutes with custom harnesses needed to be developed, tested, and manufactured in less than four weeks.

The challenge was unbelievable. Four weeks was barely enough time to produce standard product, let alone the development, testing, and manufacture of custom gear! However, John jumped at the chance.

Facing every challenge with innovative solutions, John and his team fulfilled the contract with two days to spare. Never had this been done in the history of the company.

Seeing the dedication of John and how he lead

his team, the company president decided to award him the top management post of a new division. The company who ordered the six hundred chutes had signed a contract large enough to support another manufacturing facility, and John was the new general manager.

What seemed like wasted energy and unobserved talent was noticed after all, and what seemed like an insurmountable production deadline became the path of promotion.

Let Problems Polish You

Problems can either be tools of growth or weapons of defeat; it's all in your perception of them. Let problems polish you and make you strong because inside each problem is the seed of promotion – remember David and

Goliath.

Problems can give you influence with the right people. You have pressures, adversities, and difficulties, but your **Iron Will** changes obstacles into opportunities. **Iron Will** takes difficulties and shapes them into doors that open for you.

David wondered what he would get if he killed Goliath and was promised king Saul's daughter – he would never have to pay taxes again. What motivation! David had an **Iron Will** and a purpose.

The fact that your perception of a problem can determine whether it helps you grow or brings you down is key. When you fully understand that principle, your life will take on new meaning and purpose.

President Kennedy set the United States on a course to land astronauts on the moon by the end of 1969. At that time, hardly any exploration of space had occurred and space travel to another celestial body was merely a dream.

The problems encountered by such a bold edict were formidable but not insurmountable. In fact, more advances in medicine, computer engineering, metallurgy, and other sciences resulted from the space program than from any other initiative. Problems became opportunities to arrive at creative solutions, not obstacles that derailed the train.

You Play Until You Win

People often give up before they have played the last play. It's ironic to watch professional football and pay attention to the fans. Often, the home team is behind one touchdown coming up to the end of the game.

Thinking that the game is over, people begin to clear out when there are about five minutes left on the clock. However, statistics show that more touchdowns are scored in the final two minutes than at any other time during the game. How often have the fans gone home when the winning touchdown was only seconds away?

This is not just a fan thing. Because we live in a "convenience" society – fast food, drive-through banking, the Internet, etc. – people get used to not waiting. However, patience in playing the game is important if you plan to win consistently. You cannot give up just because it looks like you may never get there. Have you reached the end of the road yet? Have you exercised your last option? Have you gone the extra mile – twice or three times? The fact is, you don't know what lies just around the next corner.

There are 3 kinds of people in the world:

- the wills – who accomplish everything
- the won'ts – who oppose everything
- the can'ts – who fail at everything

What kind of person are you? Are you willing to stick it out until the lights are turned off and the doors are locked?

If you aren't working toward something worth sticking to, then you're wasting your time. Don't expend your effort on something you don't believe in. You must have ownership of what you do in the sense that you'll not give up until the last note has been played.

If you are hard on yourself, life is easy, but if you're easy on yourself, life is hard. The choice is yours. Why not choose to pay now so you can play later?

Your Past Does Not Determine Your Future

You may have repeatedly failed at what ever you attempted to do before coming to Christ. You may have been married several times, lost a company due to mistakes in management, or been in trouble with the law. While there may some consequences that must be played out due to behavior or circumstances, the past loses its grip regarding your future. No longer are you a slave to what has been. You can be assured that the future is bright and you have a destiny

According to 1 Corinthians 5:21, you are the righteousness of God in Christ. Your sins are forgiven and you have no guilt to carry. You gave it all to Jesus and there is no condemnation in Christ – He took the sting away.

It's possible now to get on with your life and become the person that God intended you to be. Remember, problems are the seeds of promotion! Your **Iron Will** helps you stay the course and continue despite the view.

Do Not Confuse Talent With Character

Talent can take you to the top but character will keep you there. Crisis reveals what's on the inside, whether you have integrity or not. It's when you're in an emergency that your character is exposed.

Talent is often referred to as charisma, a magnetic or beckoning persona that draws people. However, charisma is often no deeper than the first layer of skin. The facade that people put on is nothing more than a con to steal you away. Yes, talent is a gift from God – so is charisma. Your gift back to God is how you use what He's given you.

The prophet Isaiah says that God lifts you out of the

fiery furnace, which means He promotes you as He watches how you handle the crisis, troubles, obstacles, and difficulties of life. How do you respond when faced with a battle of integrity? Do you behave the same whether in darkness or light? Are you the same at home as when you're out with others? Promotion comes in the middle of the war, not during peacetime. Components of an **Iron Will** include:

- self-control
- persistence
- discipline
- character
- confidence
- integrity

Don't Cast Away Your Confidence

Cast not away therefore your confidence, which hath great recompence of reward. For ye have need of patience, that, after ye have done the will of God, ye might receive the promise. For yet a little while, and he that shall come will come, and will not tarry. Now the just shall live by faith: but if any man draw back, my soul shall have no pleasure in him.

(Hebrews 10:35-38)

You need an **Iron Will**. Therefore, don't throw away your confidence and it's rich reward (patience, persistence). Confidence and persistence go together. After you have done God's will, you have crossed the finish line and won the prize. Difficulties will come and you will be tempted to draw back, but don't do it.

The devil attacks your confidence because he knows if he can neutralize you there, he's got you. He does everything he can to destroy the confidence you have in yourself and rob you of your confidence in God. If the devil distorts the image you have of yourself in God, you loose.

You are more than a conqueror; you are an overcomer. You are a child of the most-high God, beloved, blessed, and accepted. Hebrews 10:38 declares that if you loose your confidence you loose your reward and forfeit God's promise to you.

Develop Positive Knowing

You must instill confidence builders everyday of your life. Confidence builders include:

- a confession list of whom you are in Christ
- selected Scriptures that build faith

- favorite Scriptures that helped you through a trial

A powerful rhema word of God that helped me through college was Philippians 1:6: *"Being confident of this very thing, that he which hath begun a good work in you will perform it until the day of Jesus Christ."* That verse got me through college.

Goliath sought to rob David of his confidence. When Goliath looked, all he saw was a small boy with nothing but a shepherd's sling. Goliath looked at David and mocked him, while the devil sought to destroy him by using his image of himself and his covenant with God. If the devil can rob you of the right picture of yourself and God, he can steal your confidence and you'll loose your rich reward.

You must know in your knower who you are and to whom you belong. Go beyond positive thinking till you get to positive knowing. You must know who you are, who God is, and who the devil is.

Exercise Brings Confidence

When I was a youth pastor, the pastor I worked for would get me up at 6am to go jogging. I had no desire to jog or exercise, but it was part of my job description. The church was in Iowa and it can get mighty cold there, especially in winter. Each morning, we would jog to the church and pray, then go back home and take a shower before going into the office. That was a morning ritual that we did together and I felt motivated to cooperate.

One day I asked him, why in the world he did it. I'll never forget what he told me. He said it was because exercise built confidence in his life for the day at hand. Confidence is built with proper…

- Exercise
- Nutrition
- Sleep
- Association
- Reading
- Meditation
- Visualization
- Goals
- Dreams

Courage Is An Attitude of the Soul

Courage is a component of **Iron Will** that enables you to stay on course and not look to the left or the right. Courage is defined as an inward attitude expressed through bold, daring, risk-taking actions.

God instructed Joshua to conquer to the Promised

Land. However, between the wilderness and the Promised Land was Jericho, a fortified city surrounded by a great wall. God told Joshua to be strong and courageous because he would have to take a risk. God told Joshua to be bold and daring, and trust in Him and the relationship Joshua had with Him. This trust would give Joshua the courage to overcome Jericho and any other problems in his life.

> *Be strong and of a good courage: for unto this people shalt thou divide for an inheritance the land, which I swear unto their fathers to give them.*
>
> *Only be thou strong and very courageous, that thou mayest observe to do according to all the law, which Moses my servant commanded thee: turn not from it to the right hand or to the left, that thou mayest prosper whithersoever thou goest.*

> This book of the law shall not depart out of thy mouth; but thou shalt meditate therein day and night, that thou mayest observe to do according to all that is written therein: for then thou shalt make thy way prosperous, and then thou shalt have good success.
>
> (Joshua 1:6-8)
>
> That by two immutable things, in which it was impossible for God to lie, we might have a strong consolation, who have fled for refuge to lay hold upon the hope set before us.
>
> (Hebrews 6:18)

God cannot lie, and this truth must be the foundation of your faith. If it isn't, and you have even an inkling that God might not be truthful, your faith will always be weak. Faith is built on the fact that God cannot lie. Now you have a strong consolation upon which to take hold (**Iron Will**) of the hope (purpose) set before you.

Hope Is An Anchor

> *Which hope we have as an anchor of the soul, both sure and steadfast, and which entereth into that within the veil.*
>
> (Hebrews 6:19)

This hope is a stabilizing anchor (**Iron Will**) to your soul. Hope set before you brings strong determination, and causes you stay on course. Hope is the fuel of determination. Without hope, all energy to prevail is lost and the cause is defeated. Viktor E. Frankel wrote:

> *It is a peculiarity of man that he can only live by looking to the future... And this is his salvation in the most difficult moments of his existence,*

although he sometimes has to force his mind to the task.[1]

Looking to the future while being firmly grounded in the present is critical to your well-being. You must have a grasp of where you are, or you'll never know where you are going. However, knowing your destiny gives you strength and the ability to hang on when the going gets rough here and now. The book of Revelation in the Bible is one of triumph and victory. God wants you to know that the cause in which you are engaged is one that results in victory.

Likewise, as you work toward your future here, you must get past the obstacles that threaten to thwart the plan you have made. Remember, God wants you to succeed. He's not interested in keeping you poor, downtrodden, debt-ridden, or defeated. He wants you to overcome and then teach others how to do it.

Iron Will is displayed in your character; doing the things you ought to do, when you ought to do them. However, the day will come when you can live your dream and do what you want to do, when you want to do it. Success gives you more options in life.

Fight The Good Fight of Faith

The final component of an **Iron Will** is faith. How many fiery darts have been thrown at you today? If you are like other believers, you take hits every day that are meant to steal, kill, and destroy. How about the mental torment that you went through with these everyday things:

- Pressures on the job
- Long, slow lines of traffic
- Financial pressures

- The voice of the enemy

- The needs of your children

Standing tall and working through these problems is the secret of fighting the good fight. You cannot hide your head in the sand and expect things to get better. Remember, if you do put your head in the sand, a very vulnerable part of you is exposed. Therefore, stand! Just as Paul exhorted the Ephesian believers to stand after putting on the armor of God, so too, you must stand.

Standing is not only for your good but for the good of others around you. People are looking to see how you handle situations that are difficult. Will you turn and run or will you face the problem head on and fight to overcome it. Despair and worry do nothing but cause you to get sick and feel hopeless. Overcome worry and despair by remembering who is sovereign (God) and who is not (you). Then, as you stand up to the problem you will heed the advice Paul gave to Timothy:

Fight the good fight of faith, lay hold on eternal life, whereunto thou art also called, and hast professed a good profession before many witnesses.

I give thee charge in the sight of God, who quickeneth all things, and before Christ Jesus, who before Pontius Pilate witnessed a good confession.

(1 Timothy 1:12-13)

Lay hold of eternal (abundant) life with the good fight of faith. Feed your faith and starve your doubt. Create an atmosphere for your faith to grow. You'll not fulfill your calling, cross the finish line, gain the prize, overcome, be victorious, or write a story with your life unless you remain in the faith.

Don't quit. Develop an **Iron Will**. Become unstoppable and unbreakable in Jesus' name.

Pray this prayer out loud to seal the teaching in this book in your soul:

> Eternal God. You are the Sovereign Lord of the universe and You have accepted me as a child. Create in me an **Iron Will** that will enable me to overcome the pressures, trials, and temptations of life. Build within me a temple fit for Your habitation and willing to receive You. Give me strength to stand when I'm the weakest.
>
> You are my source of strength and power, Lord, so fill me now with Your Holy Spirit. Enable me to walk in His power and strength. In Jesus Mighty name. Amen.

Footnote

[1] Viktor E. Frankl, "Man's Search For Meaning" Washington Square Press, Published by Pocket Books, page 94.